CREATE and DISCOVER

A course in musical invention

Richard McNicol

Music Department
OXFORD UNIVERSITY PRESS
Oxford and New York

An Apollo Project
produced in collaboration with
The Apollo Trust, BP, and Save & Prosper

Oxford University Press, Walton Street, Oxford OX2 6DP
Oxford New York Toronto
Delhi Bombay Calcutta Madras Karachi
Petaling Jaya Singapore Hong Kong Tokyo
Nairobi Dar es Salaam Cape Town
Melbourne Auckland

and associated companies in
Berlin Ibadan

Oxford is a trade mark of Oxford University Press

© Oxford University Press 1989

All rights reserved. No part of this publication may be
reproduced, performed, stored in a retrieval system, or
transmitted, in any form or by any means, electronic,
mechanical, photocopying, recording, or otherwise, without
the prior permission of Oxford University Press or the
appropriate licensing authority

ISBN 0 19 321428 8

Contents

		page
1	**Folk-songs and drones** music from Luciano Berio *Folk Songs* (1964)	6
2	**Ostinatos and economy** music from Igor Stravinsky *The Soldier's Tale* (1918)	16
3	**Horizontal music** music from Arnold Schoenberg *Pierrot Lunaire* (1912)	22
4	**Musical impressions** music from Charles Ives *Three Places in New England* (1908–14)	26
5	**When all notes are equal** music from Anton Webern *Five Pieces for Orchestra Op. 10* (1913)	33
6	**Devil's intervals** Witold Lutosławski *Chain I* (1983)	37

Introduction

Wherever you find human beings you find music.

Music is invented by individuals and by groups. Songs and dances are still performed that were invented long ago and have been remembered and passed down from generation to generation. Some people make up new music spontaneously as they perform; others after long and painstaking labour. Music is constantly being invented, and although we in the West often notate our music, most of the world's music is not written down.

When people invent music they use skills learnt from listening. They may not realize that they possess these skills, but we all have many subconscious musical memories on which we may draw. If we enjoy inventing music and want to increase the satisfaction we get from it, we practise inventing. And just as our tennis improves when we practise the serve, the volley, and the backhand, so our musical invention or 'composition' improves when we practise various ways of putting sounds together.

Whatever people may say, there are no 'rules' to composing. There may be more or less satisfactory ways of combining sounds, but it is for us to decide what we like and what we do not like. When Beethoven, one of the most skilful Western composers ever to have lived, produced his last works for string quartet, he used combinations of notes that no one had ever used before. People were shocked and said that he was mad. Yet these quartets are now considered to be among the world's greatest masterpieces. Some of the great twentieth-century composers whose work we will explore in these projects have invented music that Beethoven might have considered quite lunatic had a composer of his time invented it. Indeed some of them faced riots at the concerts where their music was first performed. But time has proved that they had something valuable to say in their music.

These projects will introduce you to some of the ideas used by the composers of our time. Experiment with them for yourself. A lot of the pleasure in composing is simply playing with sounds. And if you are truly convinced by what you produce, then for you it is right. Enjoy it!

Richard McNicol

Chapter 1   Folk-songs and drones

This series of projects explores folk-song and one of the most ancient of all accompaniments, the drone.

A drone is simply a long, single note that accompanies a melody. It must have been one of mankind's earliest musical discoveries. Instruments which can play drones are found in folk music all over the world. Bagpipes, which allow the player to play a tune *and* hold a continuous note at the same time without running out of breath, are very popular with folk musicians. So are stringed instruments which can play rhythmical drones.

PROJECT 1   The nightingale (Rossignolet du bois)

*Video reference**
00.01

This is an old French love-song.

---

*As a general rule, project work should be completed first, and the video viewed afterwards.

00.22   **1** Find a note that you can use as a drone to accompany the song. You must decide whether to use a voice or an instrument to perform the drone. Do you want a long, held note or would you prefer a rhythmical drone? Perform the song with its drone, and record it so that you can play it back while you experiment with the next stage of the project.

01.12   **2** Can you find one note—different from the drone note—that another performer could sing or play from time to time during the song? We do not want another drone, just another note that could be slotted in occasionally. Do you want a note that fits in smoothly, or would it be interesting to use a note that clashes with part of the tune?

01.37   **3** When you have decided on this note, choose another note for the extra performer to use at other points in the song. Decide what is the most effective way to use the two notes. Will you use them as short notes or as long notes? Will your extra performer play for most of the song or just very occasionally? You may decide that each note need only be used two or three times during the whole verse.

01.59   **4** You may be satisfied with your drone and two-note accompaniment. Or you may feel that you need to add a little more. If so, choose two more notes that will fit into your accompaniment. Do not attempt to write a tune. Use them in the same way as you used the first two notes. Your new notes may fit nicely with or between the other notes. Or you may wish to alter the placing of the original notes now that you have more notes to play with.

5 Have you decided whether voices or instruments would be more effective for your four-note part? Do you still only need one extra performer, or would you like to use different sounds for some of your four notes?

02.21   **6** If you added an untuned percussion part would it improve or spoil the song?

7 When you are satisfied with your work, perform it and record it. Then you will be able to listen to the tape and decide if there are any alterations you would like to make.

PROJECT 2   **Song of sorrow (Motettu de tristura)**

03.57   A woman from Sardinia is mourning someone she loved. Every time she hears a nightingale sing she is reminded of her loss.

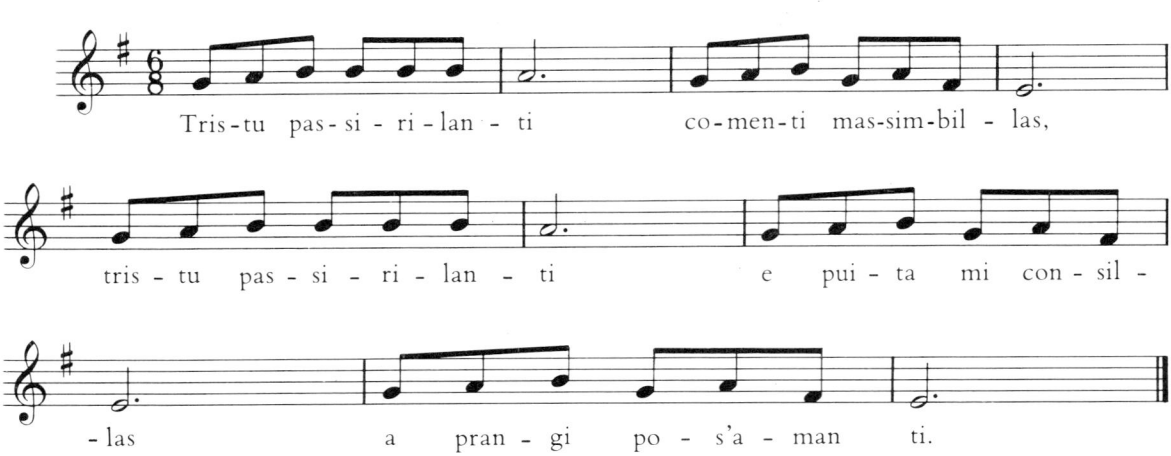

04.48   **1** The melody is extremely simple. It only uses two short phrases. You could use the last note of the song as a drone. Would it be effective to find another note to use as a double drone, or would this spoil the simplicity of the song?

05.01   **2** The singer comes from a primitive and superstitious island. Could you find a way of playing your drone that would capture a mood of primitive superstition? The sort of sound you choose will help. Should your drone be continuous or not?

06.26   **3** Could you add to this mood by using untuned percussion? You will have to be very careful with your choice of instruments. Loud rhythms would spoil the haunting quality of the song. Will you use percussion instruments often or sparingly? Should they fit with the rhythm of the song or should they be played freely?

08.09

4 The singer is reminded of her loved one when she hears the nightingale sing. Invent some bird-song using notes from this scale. If you do not read music easily, your teacher will show you which notes they are.

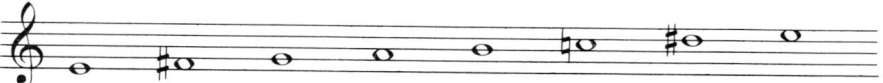

What are the characteristics of bird-song? Do birds sing a continuous flow of notes? Do they sing long or short phrases? Do they always sing something different or do they repeat phrases?

5 Which instrument would be most effective for your bird-song? Do you want it to sound like an actual bird or would you prefer to create the impression of bird-song?

6 How will you use the bird-song? Should the bird sing continuously as the song unfolds? Should it sing between verses? Perhaps you would like it to introduce the song, or perhaps you might feel that this would leave you with nothing in store for the rest of the song.

06.53 and 07.55

7 There is a strong feeling of pain in the song. Have you managed to capture this in your accompaniment? You might be able to add a stab of pain by using notes that clash with each other. Should you add a touch of stabbing bitterness to the bird-song or to any other part of your music?

08.31

8 Is your song now complete or are there any other ideas you would like to add that would make it more expressive?

9 Record your completed song and listen to it.

PROJECT 3 Sicilian song (A la femminisca)

11.35 The singer is a rough Sicilian peasant woman who sells the fish that her husband brings home in his fishing boat. She prays for his safe return (with a good catch!) in a low, husky voice.

1. E Sig - nu - ruz - zu miù fa - ci - ti bon ___ tem - pu ha iu l'a - man - ti miù 'mmez - zu lu ma - ri l'ar - vu - li d'o rue lin - tin - ni d'ar - gen - tu la Mar - un - nuz - za mi ___ l'a - v'a - iu - ta - ri.

1 Decide on a drone-note which can be used for the entire song. There may be more than one possibility. You must decide which to use.

12.03 **2** Instead of using a continuous drone, invent a way of 'colouring' your drone that will suit the song. You might colour it in a number of ways. Here are some possibilities:
- make the drone rhythmical
- use more than one sound
- give different rhythms to two or three drone performers
- 'bend' the drone by asking the performers to go sometimes above the note and sometimes below it
- change the loudness of the drone, either suddenly or gradually.

Do not forget that the drone must not drown the singer.

12.52

3 Here is a new idea to introduce when you have decided on the colour of your drone. Use a *falling scale of notes* to invent a new part for your accompaniment. Your falling scale may be part of a major scale, a minor scale, or a scale of your own invention. You may decide to use only three or four notes of your scale, or a few notes at first, adding more descending notes later in the song. Be careful not to use the scale too prominently or too often; you do not want it to sound like someone practising scales!

4 Would it improve the accompaniment if more than one performer used the downward scale idea? Should you always use the same series of notes?

5 Give careful thought to the sounds you are going to use to accompany the voice. Would a mixture of vocal and instrumental sounds be most effective or should you use one or the other only? Could you make effective use of untuned percussion?

6 The song has two verses. Should the accompaniment to the second verse be different or should it be the same as the first verse?
CAUTION   The song is simple. If your accompaniment is too complex or too 'clever' you may lose its primitive character.

7 Record and listen.

PROJECT 4   **Black is the colour**

1. Black, black, black____ is the co-lour of my true love's hair, his lips are some-thing ro-sy fair, The__ sweet - est smile and the kind - est__ hands; I love the grass where-on he stands.

14.39   In folk music, drones are most often used *underneath* the tune. But could we make effective use of a drone *above* a song, or even at the same level so that the melody threads its way around the drone, sometimes higher and sometimes lower?

1 Use an instrument or voice to sustain the first note of 'Black is the colour' while someone sings the complete song. Which do you think will best suit the mood of the song:
- a long, sustained drone?
- a drone with a regular rhythm of its own?
- a drone that follows the rhythm of the song?

Your choice may be limited by the sort of sound you want to use for the drone. If you decide on a voice, or the string of a violin, any of the above alternatives will be possible. If you feel that the sound of a xylophone is exactly what is needed for this song, the first alternative will be quite impossible!

2 Record and listen.

15.09

3 When you have decided how to perform the drone, invent another part that weaves around it. But please limit yourself to two notes on either side of the drone, E and F above it, C and B♭ below.

Invent a part that is completely independent of the song melody. It can move at its own speed and it can stop and start quite freely. Here are some possibilities. While the drone sounds your new part might:
- flicker continuously between B♭, C, E and F
- move more slowly from one note to the next
- invent a fragment of tune using these notes and play it from time to time around the drone
- invent several different fragments and alternate them
- play different pairs of notes together.

4 Should the drone note have the same sound as the other four notes or do you want to use different instruments? You will have decided whether the drone D should be rhythmical or held. Do you want to change this now that you are adding sounds around it?

15.51

5 So far, there are no really low notes in this accompaniment of 'Black is the colour'. Everything we have invented lies around the notes of the tune. Do you feel that your version needs the support of a lower part? You could provide this with an additional drone on a low D, or you might experiment with a falling scale like you used in 'A la femminisca'. Can you find a way of using a series of notes descending step by step in your version of 'Black is the colour'?
- Which note will you choose to start on?
- Which notes will you choose to be in your scale?
- How fast will it fall compared with the melody?
- Will you choose an instrument or a voice to perform it?

6 Would it add anything to the song if you added untuned percussion?

16.25

7 The mood of the song is gentle and loving. Behind these feelings lurks a distant dread—'What would I do if he died?' Can you use some of the musical ideas you have invented to capture this mood before the singer starts? Should you invent some music to go between the two verses? How are you going to finish the song?

8 Record and listen.

13

PROJECT 5   Unhappy the man (Malurous qu'o uno fenno)

This old French folk-song jokes about the universal truth that no one is ever happy. Verse 1 says: 'Unhappy the man who cannot find a wife, for he wants to be married'. Verse 2 replies: 'Unhappy is the man who is married, for he wants to be free.'

19.24   Sing the song and use a D drone *above* the melody to accompany it. The song is simple and light-hearted; it only contains two short phrases.

19.38   If we invent some melodic music to go above the drone, it should balance the song below the drone very effectively.

19.43

1 We experimented with downward scales in 'A la femminisca' and 'Black is the colour'. Use this idea again, but moving up *and* down the scale, to invent a melodic line that will sound well against the song and the drone.
- Which notes will you choose to form your scale?
- The song uses a mixture of longer and shorter notes. Perhaps your music should do the same.
- You will not need to invent a lot of music. Remember that the person who first sang the song only invented two short phrases.

19.50

2 Experiment until you have found something you like. You may feel restricted by always having to move to the next note. If you need to, use an occasional jump, perhaps to the next note but one. If you jump too often your music may become disjointed and awkward-sounding.

3 Should your music be continuous or should it sometimes stop and restart? Should it start and finish at the same time as the voice?

20.13

4 Could you take part of your music and the drone, and use them as an introduction for the song? If what you have invented sounds interesting on its own *and* fits well with the song you have succeeded very well indeed!

5 The song is bright and rhythmical. Would it benefit from some untuned percussion?

6 Record and listen.

Chapter 2 Ostinatos and economy

An ostinato is a fragment of music that is repeated continuously. The projects in this chapter use ostinatos to accompany melodies.

PROJECT 1 In the street

This is a Russian folk-song.

1. And now the snow hides, the water from the roof flies, No master in the house, And the mistress cries, There's no master in the house, And the mistress cries.

2 My dear you are
   My own true love,
   Cook a pike to make a stew
   My dearest do,
   Cook a pike to make a stew
   My dearest do.

3 Oh make a stew
   And with parsley too,
   You're my darling little maid
   And I do love you,
   You're my darling little maid
   And I do love you.

Translation by Nigel Osborne

1 Learn the song and perform it using the first four notes as a continuous ostinato to accompany your performance. What instrument might be suitable?

2 Can you find another fragment of 'In the street' that you could use as a second ostinato to accompany the song? Three notes will probably be sufficient. Perform the song again using both ostinatos at the same time.

3 An ostinato can include a period of silence between the repetitions. Can you find another section of the tune that you can repeat at intervals, so that you have three or four notes, a similar period (three or four notes-worth) of silence, then your three or four notes again, and so on throughout the song?

4 Which instruments would be suitable to play the ostinatos in a brisk, rhythmical song like this?

5 Your accompaniment may now be complete. An introduction would help the singers to find their note. Could you use one or more of the ostinatos as an introduction?

6 How will you finish the song?

7 Record a performance and listen to it. Is there anything you would like to alter?

PROJECT 2 **My little room**

Here is another Russian folk-song.

Translation by Nigel Osborne

This time you must devise your own ostinatos.

1 Invent an ostinato (not a drone) that will provide a bass for the song. A two-note ostinato will work perfectly well, or you may decide to be a bit more adventurous.

2 Find the notes for another ostinato. What sort of rhythm are you going to use? The song is an endless chattering stream of notes. Perhaps your ostinato should be slower moving with gaps between notes. Would it be a good idea to avoid the strong beats of the melody and play an off-beat ostinato?

3 When we choose notes to go with a melody we are often careful to avoid notes that clash and sound as if they 'don't fit'. If you play the adjacent notes F and F♯ together you will hear a very strong clash. Would this sort of sound add a bit of spice to 'My little room'?

4 Choice of instruments is always important. If you decide that you would like some clashing notes it will make a considerable difference which instruments you choose to play them. Try playing F and F♯ simultaneously on a pair of chime bars. Now try it on a xylophone using hard rubber beaters. Which clashes more?

5 Perform your completed piece, record it, and listen to it.

PROJECT 3 March

'In the street' and 'My little room' are continuous melodies. When we reach the end of a verse we start again and perform the next verse.

But not all music consists of continuous melody and accompaniment. In Project 3 we will compose a march, accompanied by a continuous, marching ostinato. And the march tune itself will be more dramatic than an ordinary melody. It will be made up of short interrupted phrases developed from a single musical shape.

Here is the ostinato. It consists of two notes, G and D, which alternate in the pulse of a march.

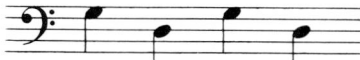

If you are unsure of the speed of a march, march across the room. The sound of your feet on the floor is the pulse of a march.

Here is the shape of the phrase that you will develop into sections of march tune. It goes down for four notes and then up for four notes.

Video reference
22.06

1 **The ostinato** You have no control over this. It must march on unaltered. Record it onto a continuous cassette, or programme it into a computer, so that you can play it while you experiment with the march phrases.

2 **March phrases** I'd like your march to portray someone in a dilemma, sometimes striding confidently forward, sometimes hesitant and unsure.

22.16

a) When I wrote the shape of the melody I purposely put no clef in front of the notes. Play the phrase shape with the ostinato. Which note are you going to choose to start on? Experiment. Do you prefer some starting notes to others? When you invent your march you may decide to start sometimes on one note and sometimes on another. Your march tune must always move to adjacent notes. No leaps are allowed.

22.20

b) What will be the rhythm of your first phrase? Should it march note for note with the ostinato? Should you have two notes of tune to each note of the ostinato? Should you have a mixture? Would smooth or jerky rhythms be more effective? What about a combination of both? Would you like your march to be 'jazzy' in character?

22.24   c) Your march should consist of a series of separate phrases over an unaltering ostinato. Can you invent an extended version of the basic phrase to use as the second phrase of your march?
You might extend it by

- playing the first two notes of the phrase twice, putting a kink into the melodic shape. Where else could you add a kink?

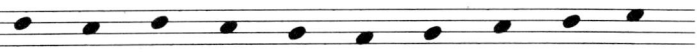

- adding extra notes to the beginning or end of the phrase
- making a false start, leaving an unexpected silence, and starting again. Could you use this device anywhere else in the phrase?

22.53   d) As you develop variations of the basic shape you might alter the relationship between phrase and ostinato. What does it sound like if you start your phrase one note later so that the ostinato is upside-down against the tune? Could you develop a phrase with notes that fit in between the pulse of the ostinato?

e) Try 'switching off' the ostinato for a while, and invent some extended phrases without it. Now add the ostinato to your new phrases. How well do they work together?

When you have invented three or four altered and extended versions of the original shape you are almost ready to assemble your march. But before you do, here is a last ingredient.

23.14   **3 Fanfares**   Fanfares were originally trumpet calls used as a flourish of sound to announce an important person, or as a signal to frighten an enemy. Invent some brief, vigorous fanfares to add to your march, using these major chords:

If you do not read music easily, your teacher will show you how to find major chords on a keyboard. Even if you do not play keyboard, sit down and explore, finding as many major chords as you can. Take your time and enjoy getting to know the sound of a major chord.

a) Fanfares should be very simple. Invent a fanfare using the notes of one major chord. If you are using very few notes, the effectiveness of your fanfare will depend on the rhythms you choose.

b) Try playing one major chord followed immediately by a different one. Some pairs of chords sound quite ordinary whilst other pairs sound exciting or even startling. Which pairs do you like? Can you invent a fanfare where the notes of one chord follow the notes of another? You might even invent a sort of sandwich-fanfare:

23.21   chord 1 – chord 2 – chord 1

c) Perhaps you wish to use other major chords not listed here.

4 Putting the march together Your march should consist of an unchanging ostinato, separated march phrases and fanfares.

a) Will you start immediately with your first phrase or would a short introduction be effective? Which of your musical ingredients would make a good introduction?

b) The ostinato should march on unaltered. Would it make your march more effective if you allowed it to rest occasionally?

c) How will you use the fanfares? Should they play during the march phrases or should they be used to punctuate the march, sounding when the tune rests?

23.57

d) The march you have invented has a tune and an ostinato. It can probably be performed by two instruments, with a third playing the fanfares. Can you invent a part for another instrument to play? This instrument will only play occasionally (it may simply play five notes and then stop), but it will help to 'fill out' the sound of your march and give it a little variety.

e) Which instruments should perform your march?

When you have completed the march, perform it, record it, and listen to it.

PROJECT 4 Dance

26.43

Here is another ostinato:

26.52
27.10

and two fragments:

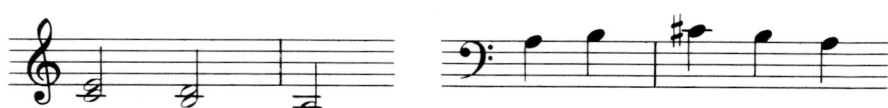

Invent a dance. As before, start by recording the ostinato or programming it into a keyboard or computer; then experiment with different ways of using the fragments. You may alter the character of the fragments and you may extend them a little if you wish. You may use up to four instruments.

Chapter 3   Horizontal music

Learning to make good use of our musical ideas is one of the most important skills in composing. In the first two chapters you invented new music to accompany melodies. Would it be possible to take a phrase and invent a complete piece of music using only the ingredients of that phrase? When somebody invents a round like 'London's burning' that is exactly what they have done. The tune is used in horizontal layers to accompany itself.

PROJECT 1

Night

Here is a musical 'idea':

It is a particularly good one because it offers all sorts of inventing possibilities. Play it for yourself. If you do not read music easily your teacher will show you how to find it on a keyboard. Will it work as a short round? Where should the second player start?

Video reference
34.46

35.17   Let's see what other musical material we can get from the phrase. Sit at a keyboard and take your time experimenting with it:

36.00   **1** Play the first three notes. You finish on the note below the one you started on. Start on this note and play the same shape. Can you go all the way down the keyboard doing this?

35.32   **2** Play the first three notes. This time drop to the fourth note of the phrase. Now repeat the pattern starting on this note. Can you continue this pattern or 'sequence'?

33.14   **3** For the next experiment you need to play two parts at once. If you are not a keyboard player, team up with a friend and work as a pair. Play the first three notes and hold the last one. Still holding it, start a second part on a different note and play the same shape, imitating the first part. If you start the second part on certain notes the imitation will clash with the held note. With other starting notes, the imitation will fit comfortably. Which do you like? Can you build up a whole series of imitations holding all of the last notes? If you use an electronic keyboard the held notes will sustain to the end.

36.31   **4** The second half of the musical idea is a chromatic scale—each successive note on the keyboard played in order. You can continue a chromatic scale until you reach the end of the keyboard. What does it sound like if one player starts down the keyboard and another follows? Does it make any difference when the second player starts? Can you do the same thing with three players starting one after the other? Try going up the keyboard instead of down.

5 Can you find any other ways of using parts of the phrase?

6 You now have quite a lot of musical material, all invented from one musical idea. Here is a poem:

Night

Monstrous, murky giant black moths
Massacred the sun's bright rays.
Like a tight shut magic book
Broods the distant sky in silence.
From the misty deep recesses
Rise up scents, destroying memory.

Monstrous, murky giant black moths
Massacred the sun's bright rays.
And from heaven, earthward bound,
Downward sink with sombre pinions
Unperceived great hordes of monsters
On the hearts and souls of mankind,
Monstrous, murky giant black moths.

Use the phrase and the musical material you have invented from it to compose your own setting of this poem. Do not invent anything new—everything must come from the phrase.

36.47

7 The words of the poem describe images in a deranged mind. Can you read the first two lines aloud with all of their strange madness? Imagine you are on stage in a theatre. The audience is in darkness in front of you. You must say the words in a way that will immediately convince them of your madness. The music you are inventing is to be performed while the poem is recited.

32.36

8 Could you use the complete phrase, or part of it, to create a feeling of darkness and fear? You might use it as a round to give an impression of layers of darkness. Or you might have different ideas. What sort of sounds are dark?

9 Some of the words seem to invite you to illustrate them with music.

> From the misty deep recesses
> Rise up scents . . .

37.24

is a good example. Did you invent any 'rising' ideas when you experimented with the phrase? '. . . in silence' might require no music at all! You must decide what will be most effective. Be careful not to be *too* obvious if you decide to illustrate words in a direct way.

10 The first two lines of the poem occur again at the beginning of the second verse or 'stanza'. And the first line appears for a third time at the end of the poem. Should you use the same music each time the same words occur?

11 Should the voice recite while the music plays or should they alternate?

37.31

12 Take care that your music does not go on at the same level for the whole poem. Many pieces of music build up to a climax. Where might the climax of this poem be?

13 When you have completed your version of 'Night' and decided which instruments to use, then perform, record, and listen to it.

PROJECT 2   **The moonfleck**

Here is another poem from the same set as 'Night', by the Belgian poet Albert Giraud. Pierrot, a simple-minded character from French pantomime, is affected by moon-madness.

The moonfleck

With a snowy fleck of shining moonlight
On the shoulder of his black silk frock-coat,
So walks out Pierrot this languid evening
Seeking everywhere for love's adventure.

But what, something's wrong with his appearance.
He looks round and round and then he finds it,
Just a snowy fleck of shining moonlight
On the shoulder of the black silk frock-coat.

Wait now, thinks he, 'tis a piece of plaster.
Wipes and wipes yet cannot make it vanish,
So he goes on poisoned with his fancy,
Rubs and rubs until the early morning,
Just a snowy fleck of shining moonlight.

Here are the ingredients you may use to invent music to perform with the poem. You may use them in any octave you wish.

1 Imagine the poem is going to be spoken. Invent a little march for an instrument to accompany the words, using only the notes in the first group (A).

2 Remember the march you invented in Chapter 2. Should your new march be continuous, or a series of rather disjointed phrases? It will not need to 'fit' with the words, but perhaps it could be played while they are spoken to help us to feel more strongly the way Pierrot feels. Could you make it 'languid'? Don't forget that the moon has affected Pierrot and made him behave strangely.

3 Do you want your melody to illustrate any of the words? 'A snowy fleck of shining moonlight' might deserve special attention. But take care! Too much illustration of words might spoil the simple elegance of the mood.

4 Can you invent a rhythmical accompaniment to your march using the three notes in the B group? Do you want the notes to fit beautifully with the march tune or would you like them to sound a little strange?

5 In the second stanza Pierrot gets very confused. Do you remember, earlier in this chapter, exploring the idea of phrases imitating themselves? Could you use that technique to convey Pierrot's confusion? For example:

40.30
    a) How would your march sound if you treated it as a round? You might record it and play it back, playing the second part of the round yourself. Could you add a third part?

41.34
    b) Would it be effective to treat your rhythmic accompaniment in the same way? You will need some more players or a multi-track recorder so that you can experiment.

    c) Do you need to add other new instruments in this middle section? Are you going to illustrate any words?

6 So, Pierrot walks on, as in the beginning of the poem, but his evening, and the balance of his mind, are in some way 'poisoned'. Could you create a 'poisoned' version of your opening music for this stanza? Or should you invent something different?

7 How are you going to fit the words and music together?

8 Perform 'The moonfleck', record it, and listen to it.

CHAPTER 4　Musical impressions

When we listen to *Pierrot Lunaire* we are freed from any worries about what sounds 'right' and what sounds 'wrong'. At first you may think it all sounds wrong! But you will soon get used to the sound of Schoenberg's music and I hope you will appreciate how effectively it captures the mad world of Pierrot.

Once we cease to worry whether our music sounds 'right' and become confident enough simply to invent what *we* think is effective, we can use music in all sorts of imaginative ways.

Video reference
44.38

44.46

Watch the beginning of Programme 4 of the video and concentrate on the shots of the River Thames and the Houses of Parliament. Look at the fine detail in the film. Now look at Monet's painting of the scene as it looked in his day. Monet was perfectly capable of painting the kind of detail you can see in the film. But he was not interested in detail. He wanted to use his painting skills to show something quite different. He wanted to capture an *impression* of the scene in fading light.

PROJECT 1　Party piece

44.53

Now watch the next scene on the video. When we made the video we had an end-of-shoot party. In the middle of it, I dropped a glass. There was a shocked silence, and some bits of broken glass hit the clarinettist (fortunately she wasn't hurt); then the party gradually returned to normal.

Painters are not the only people who can create impressions. Use the party scenario as an idea for a short piece of music. Here are some questions that may help you:

- When someone is talking and you cannot quite hear the words, what can you hear? Are the sounds all the same length or are they a mixture of different lengths? Do they have any rhythm?
- Are they all exactly the same loudness or are there different degrees of loudness and softness?
- Is speech continuous or does it stop and start?
- Do all the sounds seem to be on the same note or do they go up and down in pitch?

You might tackle the first question by inventing a sentence, recording it, and listening carefully to it:

'Yesterday, as I was coming home . . .'

When I say it, I make a mixture of long and short sounds, like this:

. . —   . . . . —

and my speech has a lilting rhythm.

1 Take an instrument and play the rhythm of your sentence. Then forget about speech and see if you can extend that rhythm using similar rhythms.

2 Now apply the answers to the other questions to what you have just invented, adding loudness and softness, stops and starts, and pitch. When you have finished you will have musical phrases that owe their origin to the patterns of speech. But they are no longer impersonating speech—they are musical phrases in their own right.

3 If you are working on your own, invent some more phrases. Remember that all voices sound different. How can you translate this into music? If you are working in a group, listen to other people's phrases.

4 Now assemble the phrases. If you are on your own you will need a multi-track recorder. When a roomful of people talk it can make a meaningless jumble of sound. Don't forget that you are assembling a piece of music. Organize the overlapping phrases carefully. It might be advisable to have no more than three playing at any one time.

5 The dropped glass is simply an idea to give a climax to the piece. Can you invent something musical that will serve the same purpose?

6 At a party there is often a record or a tape playing. If people are just talking to each other they do not listen to the music; it is simply there as a background cushion of sound to avoid awkward silences and to encourage people to relax and talk. Would it be effective to use a cushion of sound to support your music? You could use a well-known tape, playing it so quietly that it hardly filters through your conversation music. Or you could invent your own cushion, perhaps using the sounds you can get from an electronic keyboard or a synthesizer. The effectiveness of your piece may well depend on your skill in finding the right balance between the background tape and the foreground conversation phrases.

7 Perform, record, and listen to your completed piece. Is it effective as music?

PROJECT 2   A modern summer evening

Imagine you live in a road where the houses and their gardens are very close together. On a warm summer evening you can sit in your garden and listen to the sounds coming from the gardens and open windows around you. Create a piece of music that captures the atmosphere of 'A modern summer evening'.

1 To get an impression of this sort of complex sound-picture, stand in the middle of the school playground at the end of break and listen to the sounds around you. You can also hear a variety of sounds made by the people in the playground. Can you also hear other sounds? Are the sounds constant or do they sweep around you as you walk across the playground? What happens to the sounds when break ends? Do they disappear suddenly or gradually? Which sounds are left when everyone has gone back into class?

2 Imagine what you might hear sitting in the summer garden listening to the sounds all around you. Make a collection of sounds on tape that you could use to construct your 'summer evening music'.

3 Assemble your collection of sounds to make a background tape. You will have to decide how long each sound should be. Should you adjust the volume to make all your collected sounds equally loud, or should some be louder and some softer; what order should you use them in; should you use any of them more than once? What effect do you want the tape to have on the listener? Do you want to lull the audience with gentle sounds, or gradually get louder and more dramatic? Would you like to surprise or even startle? You might even want a completely random order for your collected sounds. You may have multi-track equipment at school. Would it be effective to mix the sounds? Should one sound fade into another or should sounds interrupt one another?

4 Your completed tape may be an effective piece on its own, or you may decide to use it as a background over which you can perform 'live'. Can you invent some chords and sections of melody that blend with the tape to add to the listener's impression of the quiet warmth of the evening? You might even add fragments of music that would stir a moment of recognition in the listener's mind. But be careful how you do it. A few notes of a child in a neighbouring house playing the recorder might be magical. But if you suddenly play the whole of 'Frère Jacques' you can be sure that your audience will laugh and the whole mood will be lost.

5 When your music has captured this peaceful atmosphere of warm darkness and distant, half-familiar sounds, it might be effective to shatter the peace with some loud, well-known sound. Should it be music or some other sound? What sort of loud interruption might you get on a summer night? Should it start softly and get louder, or should it suddenly burst into your quiet music? Should it be on another tape, or should you perform it live? Should it happen early or late in the piece? How long should it be? Should it stop suddenly or die away? How will you finish your complete piece?

6 Perform, record, and listen to your 'A modern summer evening'.

PROJECT 3   Dream music

The techniques you used in the first two projects in this chapter are similar to the technique we use in art when we make a collage. In the first project you invented your own collage material; in the second you assembled sounds collected on tape. In this project, make a collage with music borrowed from someone else. Here is your material:

Swanee River

Free Americay

Both are well-known American songs. The first is by Stephen Foster; the second was 'borrowed' from Britain during the American War of Independence. Imagine that these two songs featured in one of your dreams. Can you invent some 'Dream music' using only material from these songs?

1 Remember how you developed musical ideas from the 'Night' phrase in Chapter 3. What sort of musical material can you invent from parts of 'Free Americay'? It is a bright march tune. Will you use it in the military style for which it was originally intended or will you change its character? This might depend on your dream: does it have

46.40

a story-line, or is it a series of fragmented impressions cut like a film? Should you keep the fragments of 'Free Americay' at their original speed or not? Should they be exact fragments or could some of the notes or rhythms be altered to make them more dream-like? Should you use one fragment at a time or might it be effective to overlap them or fade one into another?

2 The famous American composer Charles Ives wrote that his father used to play an accompaniment to 'Swanee River' in the key of C and challenge him to sing the tune in the key of E♭ (starting on G instead of E). Here it is. Can *you* do it?

Ives' father did this to 'stretch' his son's ears—to show him the strange new and beautiful chords you can discover by experimenting.

Instead of playing or singing 'Swanee River' straight through, try playing the left-hand chords with only the melody note that lies immediately above them. If, as above, you use the C version of the accompaniment with the E♭ version of the tune, you get some very interesting chords. You might try making some of these chords even more interesting by playing the left-hand chord and adding *all* of the melody notes that lie above it at the same time. The first chord would be quite ordinary:

The second chord would be very strange indeed:

3 Experiment. Some of these chords seem ugly to me if I play them loudly on a hard-sounding instrument like a xylophone (using hard rubber beaters). Yet if the same chords are played softly on a mellow instrument—an electronic keyboard, a metallophone with soft beaters, or on stringed instruments—they can sound beautiful and mysterious. What chords could you get if you started the tune on another different note?

4 Using a tape recorder, or a multi-track recorder if available, record your own backing-track of chords from 'Swanee River'. Perhaps you should use a soft sound from an electronic keyboard to play them. Should the chords have a pulse or should they simply move freely from one long chord to the next? Should you just use chords from 'Swanee River' or would it be effective to use fragments of the tune as well?

47.25
(chords at 47.46)

5 Now experiment with fragments of 'Free Americay', performing them over the top of the backing-track. You might use layers of fragments as Schoenberg does in 'The moonfleck'. You might also use fragments of the 'Swanee River' tune.

48.17

6 Be careful that your music does not become a shapeless mess! Perhaps it should gradually build up to a climax. Would you do this by getting louder, by adding more layers of fragments, or by a combination of both? Perhaps you can find a different way of giving shape to your music.

48.43

7 When you have decided what material to use and how to combine it with the chords, you will have to make some decisions about performance. Which instruments would be most suitable for your music? You may decide to use voices; after all, you are using two songs. All the performers will need to know exactly how loudly or softly to perform.

8 Record your 'Dream music' and listen to it. Are there any improvements you would like to make?

PROJECT 4   **Carnival parade**

All over the world people celebrate special events or special days with carnivals. They dress up, they build floats and they parade through the streets accompanied by music.

Imagine you are watching a carnival parade. As each float passes you hear its music. But you can also still hear the music of the previous float, and you can begin to hear the music of the next one as it approaches. If you were to stand at a place where the procession turned back on itself, you might be able to hear four or five different pieces of music at the same time! Invent a piece of music that captures an impression of this atmosphere.

1 With a group of four or five friends make an arrangement of 'Free Americay' to perform to the rest of the class. It need not be too complicated. Someone will need to play the tune. You may decide to use the whole tune or just the first half of it. Can you find ostinatos that will accompany the first half? Each ostinato need only use two notes. If you decide to use the complete tune you may need to modify the ostinatos for the second half. Which instruments will you use to play your march?

2 Ask other members of the class to contribute some music to the procession. Should they arrange other march tunes? What other sorts of music would you expect to hear in a carnival parade? Do all floats have live music played by live musicians? Could you use some recorded music?

50.04, 51.30   3 Can you combine the different groups to create a carnival atmosphere? Should each group play continuously? How could you give the impression of different floats passing by, of their music getting closer and then further away?

4 How should your carnival music begin? Would it be most effective to start everyone at once, or could you invent a quiet cushion of music that would set the atmosphere for the parade? How should the piece finish?

5 Perform, record and listen.

CHAPTER 5 When all notes are equal

The projects in Chapter 4 aimed to encourage you to create music in which detail was less important than the overall effect of the complete piece. In this chapter the aim is precisely the opposite.

PROJECT 1 **Voices of the drowned**

Here is a poem by the Japanese poet Taigi who lived from 1709 to 1772:

> Thunder –
> voices of the drowned
> in sunken ships.

The best of these tiny 'haiku' poems are admired for the way they can create a vivid picture using (in the original Japanese) only 17 syllables.

Here are six notes:

Create a musical version of the Japanese poem. Do not use the words: yours is to be a musical parallel to the poem, not a setting of it. It must not last longer than 15 seconds, and the notes must be used in 'tone-row' order: your teacher will explain this.

1 The poet used the fewest words possible to write the poem. But they were chosen with tremendous care. I have chosen your notes.
Use them as sparingly as you can and think carefully about
  a) at which octave to use each note,
  b) the length of each note,
  c) the way you are going to combine the notes (it is surprising how many options you have with so few notes and with such strict rules),
  d) the colour of each note – which instrument will you choose to play it?

2 Each line of the poem contains a different number of syllables, there is no regular rhythm, and there are no rhyming words. Perhaps your music should have no pulse.

3 Read the poem aloud and try to express its mood and meaning. Does it help to make your voice rise and fall? Would it be appropriate for your music to rise and fall in the same shape?

4 When the poet has said what he wants to, he stops. No words are wasted and there is no 'filling out'. Think the same way about your music.

5 When you have completed your haiku, record it and listen to it.

PROJECT 2   **Openings**

Here are twelve notes. They are all different.

I have invented two phrases of keyboard music. They are as different as I can make them, but both use these twelve notes in order.

1 Can you continue each phrase, starting again at the beginning of the row of notes and keeping the same mood as I have started? Although I have used the notes in order, I have been particularly careful which ones I chose for the melody and which I chose for the chords. In the first fragment I wanted a shapely, elegant melody and gentle chords. In the second I wanted something sharp and aggressive.

2 Invent some opening phrases of your own. How different from mine can you make them?

PROJECT 3 Miniatures

Here are some more haiku:

Contending –
temple bell,
winter wind.
Kito (1740–89)

Summer grasses,
all that remains
of soldiers' dreams.
Basho (1644–94)

First cicada:
life is
cruel, cruel, cruel.
Issa (1763–1827)

Barn's burnt down –
now
I can see the moon.
Masahide (1657–1723)

Wintry day,
on my horse
a frozen shadow.
Basho

Shrine gate
through morning mist –
a sound of waves.
Kikaku (1661–1707)

Invent your own rows using all 12 notes and compose musical versions of these poems. As an example, I have used the row from Project 2 to compose my own version of the 'Thunder' haiku.

I have written my musical haiku for piano.
Notice how careful I have been:
- I have indicated the exact speed (60 crotchets to a minute) and the exact length of each note.
- I have indicated how loudly or softly each note should be played.
- I have matched the three lines of the poem, giving each a different speed:
  'Thunder' ♩ = 60
  'voices of the drowned'   poco più mosso (a little faster)
  'in sunken ships'   meno mosso, rit. (slower, getting slower still)

1 When you are deciding how to use your twelve notes, think again of the colours of the different instruments you might use. The moon poem might call for a single silver note. On which instrument? And which instrument(s) would be most suitable for the burnt-out barn below it?

2 The sounds of actual words in the poems might give you ideas. How do you think the cicada got its name? How could you make use of it in your piece?

3 How could you convey the absolute stillness of a shrine gate seen through mist?

Try to have a complete idea of your miniature before you start arranging notes. Do not just make it up as you go along.

PROJECT 4 — Sound within silence

The haiku poems were a way of giving you ideas for your music. Many composers invent music without the stimulus of non-musical ideas.

1 Take 30 seconds of silence. That may sound ridiculous, but simply sit for 30 seconds and listen to silence. You will have great difficulty doing this in our modern world. Silence is almost impossible to find, as you will discover.

Video reference
58.45

2 However, think of the silence as a sort of picture frame into which you are going to place 30 seconds-worth of sounds (and silences) selected with the *greatest* care. Each note must be as effective as you can make it in company with its neighbouring notes. No note must be wasted or put in just to fill up the time.

3 Use a 12-note row to create this 30-second piece. You may need to go through the row two or three times and you may wish to 'bend' the rules a little.

4 Think carefully about the effect you are creating. The possibilities are literally endless. Here is the beginning of a list:
   a) high notes may contrast with low notes
   b) loud notes with soft notes
   c) long notes with short notes
   d) rough sounds with smooth sounds
   e) you may want no contrast at all—everything sounding as similar as possible
   f) there may be no pulse at all (I prefer the word 'pulse' to 'beat')
   g) a fast pulse may suddenly contrast with a slow pulse
   h) a pulse may speed up
   i) a pulse may slow down
   and so on.

59.11

If this idea of putting sounds into a silence seems hard to understand, watch the video and see how the Viennese composer Webern does it. But try to invent your own music first, and then see what Webern does.

CHAPTER 6 Devil's intervals

Sit at a keyboard and play F and the B above it simultaneously. Are you horrified by the sound? I thought not! Yet if you had lived 500 years ago you would have avoided sounding these two notes together at all costs. Musicians living in those days found the clash of these notes so unbearable that they called the interval 'the devil in music'. We call it an augmented 4th.

Experiment at the keyboard until you can find augmented 4ths easily. Take your time—it does not matter if you are not a keyboard player. And listen to the distinctive sound of this interval.

Here is a game to help you to familiarize yourself with augmented 4ths.
a) Play any note.
b) Play another note an augmented 4th away.
c) Move to an adjacent note.
d) Then go back another augmented 4th.
e) What is the next note in the sequence?

You should be able to go all the way up or down the keyboard like this.

Here is another familiarity game, using the augmented 4th and the chromatic scale (which you used in 'Night' in Chapter 3).
a) Play a note, and then an augmented 4th above it.
b) Now come back part of the way chromatically (playing every note, black and white, in order).
c) Then leap another augmented 4th and repeat the pattern exactly.
d) Can you continue the sequence until you reach the end of the keyboard?

Can you invent other sequences using the augmented 4th and the chromatic scale? If you play another instrument, can you find augmented 4ths on that?

When you are familiar with augmented 4ths and chromatic scales, start using them to invent melodies. We shall make this your starting point in creating a piece of music.

Video reference
70.27

1 Invent a short, thoughtful melody using only augmented 4ths and the chromatic scale. Your melody need not have a steady pulse.

2 Using exactly the same notes, but altering anything else you like (the note-lengths, the rhythm, the dynamics), transform your melody into a brisk march. If your original melody had no pulse, you will now have to give it a steady beat. What other alterations will you have to make to it?

3 Now change it into a lullaby. Remember that a lullaby is a gentle rocking-song sung by a mother to soothe her baby to sleep. What sort of rhythm would it use?

4 In Chapter 2 you developed phrases by repeating fragments and finding other ways of extending the material you had already invented. Can you extend your new melody in this way?

5 It is very restricting to be limited to augmented 4ths and chromatic scales when you are inventing melody. It rules out any of the big melodic leaps which can make a tune both expressive and dramatic. Here are two wide intervals:
   a) Choose any note on the keyboard and play it with its 'twin' an octave higher. Now move the top note one key closer to the bottom note. This interval is called a major 7th. (You can, of course, keep the top note where it is and move the bottom note one key closer).
   b) Play the original two notes an octave apart, but this time move one of the notes one key further away from the other. This interval is a minor 9th.

Experiment until you are familiar with these intervals, then use them (either or both of them: experiment to find what sounds most effective) together with the augmented 4th and the chromatic scale to invent some more melodies (stages 6–9). It is helpful to remember that the second note of these wide intervals will always be an octave away from the first note, plus or minus one key.

72.01

6 Using only minor 9ths, major 7ths, augmented 4ths and the chromatic scale, invent a melody that might accompany a character in a Western film riding into town.
   - Try to capture the character's personality in your melody. Is he or she cool, mean and unpredictable, elegant, rough and vicious, jaunty?
   - Will the character affect your choice of leaps and close-together notes in the melody?
   - Will it affect the speed you choose?
   - What sort of rhythm will be most effective? Could an elegant person and a mean and unpredictable person be portrayed using the same sort of rhythm?
   - Will your melody be the same loudness from beginning to end or will you vary your dynamics?

7 Invent a melody to accompany somebody creeping into the same Western town under cover of darkness. Could you make effective use of wide intervals to create a feeling of the unexpected?

8 Invent a funeral march.
   - A funeral march has a steady pulse like any other march. In what way is it different?
   - Will the sorrowful seriousness of the melody call for many leaps or few?
   - Will you use varied rhythms or repetitive rhythms?

9 Invent a melody for the sheer beauty of its shape.

10 Next we must think about accompanying these melodies. In Chapter 4 you examined the idea of a cushion of sound accompanying a melody. In Project 3 you found new chords by playing the tune of 'Swanee River' in one key over an accompaniment in another. Combinations of augmented 4ths, major 7ths and minor 9ths should give some intriguing chords. Experiment at the keyboard. Start by playing F and B with your right hand. With your left hand add other augmented 4ths, major 7ths and minor 9ths, just to see what you come up with. You do not have to be able to play keyboard. Just take your time and enjoy experimenting.

11 When you have found some chords you like, record them. Choose interesting chords as well as beautiful ones. You may find a use for some harsh-sounding chords later. Make each chord long enough on the tape to give you a chance to experiment with parts of your melodies over it. If you have an electronic keyboard this will be no problem. If you are using a piano you may have to play each chord several times to make it a useful length on the recording.

72.32   **12** Now that you have a selection of chords on tape, try fitting some of them under the melodies you have invented. There are no 'rights' and 'wrongs' about whether the melody fits. It is for you to decide whether it is effective or not.

73.29   **13** You can also produce chords from the chromatic scale. Try playing three adjacent notes simultaneously. This sort of chord, where you play a clump of notes together, is usually called a 'cluster'. How does it sound if you play a cluster of three notes with one hand, miss a few notes, then add another cluster further along the keyboard? If you play clusters at the bass end of the keyboard, the sound is dark and muddy. What other possibilities are there?

73.42
to
77.26
↓

14 Some of the melodies you have produced using augmented 4ths, major 7ths, minor 9ths and bits of chromatic scale must sound quite dramatic. Your chords may also sound dramatic in themselves, but your choice of notes need not be the only dramatic thing about them. For a start, you could colour your chords and bring them to life.

    a) Take one of the chords you discovered at the keyboard. Instead of playing it yourself, ask some friends to take one note each. Choose carefully which instruments they use—you want your chord to sound well-balanced. If they play different sorts of

		instruments, this will colour the chord. Experiment to see how many different effective colours you can find for one chord.
73.23	b)	If you ask your friends to repeat their notes as fast as they can, you will give your chord a different texture. Can you find other ways of altering the texture?
75.34	c)	Instead of giving each player one note of the chord, invent a different short phrase for each to play using all the notes of the chord. If all the phrases are played simultaneously, you will still have the chord (all the notes will be there), but in a new, dramatic form. And with skilful use of dynamics it could be more dramatic still. The players simply repeat their phrases for as long as you need the chord.
77.27	d)	If you gave each player the *same* phrase, you could ask them to play it as a round. You could give the phrase an exact rhythm and specify when each player should start. Or you could decide the order of the notes and leave everything else to the individual player. Which would be more effective?
73.29	e)	How could you use individual players to bring clusters of notes to life?

Now assemble your piece of music, using the materials you have developed. Make use of their great dramatic potential. And think very carefully about the decisions you make. The great Polish composer Witold Lutosławski once said in an interview:

'Even the minutest detail should satisfy the composer's sensitivity to the maximum degree. In other words, there should be no indifferent sounds in music'.   Varga, *Lutosławski Profile* (Chester Music)